LUNGS
HEART & BLOOD

by
STEVE PARKER
Consultant
DR KRISTINA ROUTH

HOW TO USE THIS BOOK

This book is your guide to yourself – an atlas of the human body. Follow the main text to get an informative overview of a particular area of the body, or use the boxes to jump to a specific area of interest. Finally, there are even experiments for you to try yourself!

Body Locator

The highlighted areas on the body locator tell you immediately which areas of the body you are learning about. This will help you to understand your body's geography.

Instant Facts

This box gives you snappy facts that summarise the topic in just a few sentences. Find out how many times the heart beats per minute, how much blood is pumped around the body in a lifetime and much more.

Healthwatch

Go here to read about illness and disease related to the relevant area of the body. For example, on the section about blood, learn how too many fatty foods can damage our arteries.

Diagrams

Go to this box for scientific diagrams complete with annotations that tell you exactly what you are looking at.

ⓘ INSTANT FACT

If the body was as big as a large city like London or New York, **its main blood vessels would be like motorways 150 metres across,** and its tiniest vessels would be about the width of a pencil.

The heart, blood and all the blood vessels make up about 1/10th **of the weight of the whole body.**

If all the blood vessels in the body could be joined end to end, **they would go around the world more than twice.**

👁 HEALTHWATCH

What we eat, drink and do every day all have huge effects on our heart and blood vessels. Smoking, too much food rich in animals fats, lack of exercise and being overweight cause big problems. They are known as 'risk factors' for heart disease. Each risk factor on its own has a bad effect, and two or more combined make the risk to your health much worse.

HEART *ENGINE OF LIFE*

Our body has one bag-shaped muscle which cannot relax, and which must keep working all costs. This is the heart, the muscle-power pump for the circulatory system. It beats eve second to force blood through the network of blood ves

ROUND AND ROUND Our blood goes around and around, or circulates, through the body. It delivers oxygen to all body parts, organs and tissues. Blood also carries hundreds of other substances. These include energy-packed sugars, nutrients for growth, vitamins and minerals to keep the body working well, disease-fighting microscopic white cells, and the 'messenger' substances known as hormones which control many bodily processes.

ALWAYS BUSY Blood not only delivers – it collects too. It gathers up wastes for removal by other body parts. These are the two lungs, which get rid of the waste carbon dioxide, and the two kidneys, which filter unwanted substances from the blood to form the liquid urine. Blood also helps to keep our bodies at a regular temperature. It spreads heat from hard-working parts, like the heart and muscles, to cooler areas. If the body gets too hot, more blood flows through the skin and loses the extra warmth to the surroundings.

ANY KIND OF MOVEME means muscles work harder, and need extr supplies of oxygen and energy. So the heart pu harder and faster to increase blood flow through the muscles.

CONTENTS

In Focus

This panel takes a really close look at one aspect of the human body, using stunningly detailed macro-imagery and stills taken from an anatomically correct digital model of human anatomy.

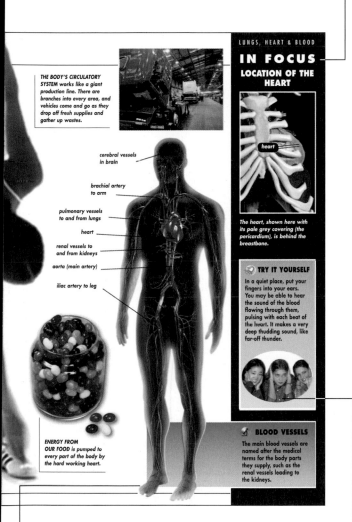

THE BODY'S CIRCULATORY SYSTEM works like a giant production line. There are branches into every area, and vehicles come and go as they drop off fresh supplies and gather up wastes.

cerebral vessels in brain

brachial artery to arm

pulmonary vessels to and from lungs

heart

renal vessels to and from kidneys

aorta (main artery)

iliac artery to leg

ENERGY FROM OUR FOOD is pumped to every part of the body by the hard working heart.

LUNGS, HEART & BLOOD

IN FOCUS
LOCATION OF THE HEART

The heart, shown here with its pale grey covering (the pericardium), is behind the breastbone.

TRY IT YOURSELF

In a quiet place, put your fingers into your ears. You may be able to hear the sound of the blood flowing through them, pulsing with each beat of the heart. It makes a very deep thudding sound, like far-off thunder.

BLOOD VESSELS
The main blood vessels are named after the medical terms for the body parts they supply, such as the renal vessels leading to the kidneys.

Try it Yourself

Activity boxes with exercises that you can try yourself. No special equipment required – just your own body!

INTRODUCTION

Astronauts, firefighters in smoke-filled buildings and deep-sea divers have one vital feature in common – their own air supply. The human body cannot last for a few minutes without taking in the substance oxygen, found in the air around us. But breathing fresh air into the lungs is only half the story. Once the oxygen is inside, it must then spread all around the body, to every tiny nook and cranny. This is the job of the heart and blood.

NEVER BREATH-LESS Parts of the body that work together for one major purpose or function are known as a body system. Taking essential oxygen into the body is the task of the respiratory system. This includes the air passages through the nose and throat, down the windpipe, to the airways and lungs in the chest. Oxygen demand is never-ending. We must breathe every few seconds of every minute, every day – and all night too.

NEVER BEAT-LESS In the lungs, oxygen passes to the circulatory system. This consists of a central pump, the heart, the blood vessels or tubes that branch from it and the blood flowing through these vessels. Like breathing, the heartbeat is non-stop, day and night, year after year. Blood delivers around the body not only the all-important oxygen, but a host of other substances needed for life and health.

When we are active, our bodies have to work harder. They take in more oxygen as we breathe faster, and our heart pumps blood round our bodies more quickly.

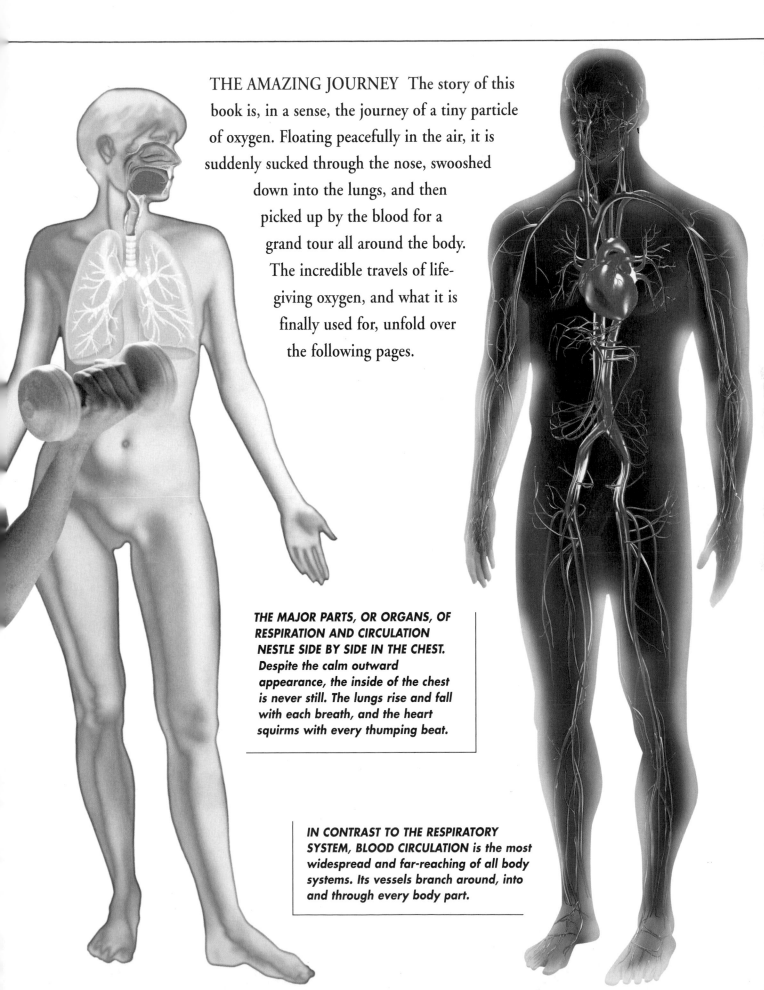

THE AMAZING JOURNEY The story of this book is, in a sense, the journey of a tiny particle of oxygen. Floating peacefully in the air, it is suddenly sucked through the nose, swooshed down into the lungs, and then picked up by the blood for a grand tour all around the body. The incredible travels of life-giving oxygen, and what it is finally used for, unfold over the following pages.

THE MAJOR PARTS, OR ORGANS, OF RESPIRATION AND CIRCULATION NESTLE SIDE BY SIDE IN THE CHEST. *Despite the calm outward appearance, the inside of the chest is never still. The lungs rise and fall with each breath, and the heart squirms with every thumping beat.*

IN CONTRAST TO THE RESPIRATORY SYSTEM, BLOOD CIRCULATION *is the most widespread and far-reaching of all body systems. Its vessels branch around, into and through every body part.*

5

The total amount of air in the respiratory system is about **4 litres in a smaller adult**, up to 6 litres in a larger adult.

The nose, throat and windpipe **hold about 0.2 litres (200 ml) of air.**

About 1 litre of air always stays in the lungs, no matter how hard we breathe out.

In an average lifetime a person takes around **half a billion breaths**.

HEALTHWATCH

Each year, more than 4 million litres of air pass in and out of the respiratory system. Its self-cleaning passageways can get rid of normal amounts of dust and particles. But very dusty or smoky air, or floating bits of powder and dirt, can cause great damage. People wear air-filter masks to trap the particles before they are breathed in and clog up the system.

LUNGS *MANY AIRWAYS*

Breathe in deeply through your nose. What can you smell? Perhaps a scent or deodorant, maybe air-freshener or flowers, even a 'people' odour of clothes and sweat. As you breathe in, oxygen begins a journey through your respiratory system, which could end at your fingers and toes!

NEED FOR OXYGEN The main purpose of the respiratory system is to get oxygen into the body. Oxygen is a gas that makes up about one-fifth of the air. It is needed in the body because it takes part in a process where glucose, a type of sugar, is broken apart to release the energy it contains. This process occurs many times every second, in every microscopic cell of the body. It is called cellular respiration. The energy it releases is then available to power the cell's hundreds of other life processes. It can be confusing, because the action of breathing is also called respiration.

WE CAN BREATHE in through the nose and mouth. The nose is more specialized to take in air, while the mouth is usually seen as part of the digestive system.

POISONOUS WASTE Our cells need a continuous supply of oxygen. When they use oxygen, however, cells make a gas called carbon dioxide. This would be poisonous if it built up inside the body. The respiratory system gets rid of the carbon dioxide. Our respiratory system also helps us in other ways. It helps with our sense of smell, and also with the power of speech.

THE INNER LININGS OF THE AIRWAYS and lungs are moist. As air comes out it carries this dampness as water vapour. When the air around is cold, the vapour condenses or turns back into tiny droplets of water – 'cold steam'.

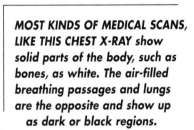

MOST KINDS OF MEDICAL SCANS, LIKE THIS CHEST X-RAY show solid parts of the body, such as bones, as white. The air-filled breathing passages and lungs are the opposite and show up as dark or black regions.

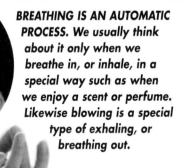

BREATHING IS AN AUTOMATIC PROCESS. We usually think about it only when we breathe in, or inhale, in a special way such as when we enjoy a scent or perfume. Likewise blowing is a special type of exhaling, or breathing out.

IN FOCUS
AIRWAYS AND LUNGS

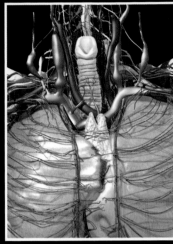

A front view reveals the voice-box at the top of the windpipe, and how high the lungs extend.

AIRWAYS

The main passage for air in the respiratory system is through the nose, around the rear of the palate to the throat, and down the windpipe to the lungs in the chest.

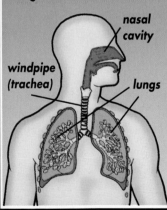

nasal cavity

windpipe (trachea)

lungs

TRY IT YOURSELF

How many ways can you breathe out? Often we use out-breaths to show our thoughts and emotions in an unspoken way. You could breathe out softly as a sigh of sadness, or slightly harder when you give up on a problem, or harder still to show irritation.

On average, the inside of the nose makes about **enough mucus every day to fill two egg-cups.**

During normal breathing, air flows in and out of the nose at about **2 metres per second.**

During a cough it rushes out of the mouth **at 20 metres per second.**

During a sneeze it **blasts out of the nose at 30 metres per second.**

HEALTHWATCH

Some people have an allergy or sensitivity to tiny floating particles in air, like dust or plant pollen. The lining inside the nose tries to 'fight' these particles as if they were harmful germs. The lining becomes swollen and itchy with runny nose and sneezing. The general name for this condition is allergic rhinitis. Allergy to pollen is sometimes called 'hay fever'.

LUNGS *Upper Airways*

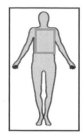

Sniff, sniff, blow ... when you have a cold, or go out in the windy winter sun, or shed a few tears, your nose may drip or run. It needs a good blow into a paper tissue or handkerchief to clear it. A runny nose can be annoying. But the slimy, sticky mucus has a vital job, to protect the delicate lining from drying out and thus preventing attack by germs.

INSIDE THE NOSE The nose is the body's air-conditioning unit. It warms, moistens and filters incoming air. The nose's two holes, nostrils, lead into twin air spaces just behind the nasal chambers. Each is bigger than a thumb and has a lining which is damp with mucus and also rich in tiny blood vessels. As the air flows in, it is warmed and moistened, which makes it better prepared to enter the very delicate lungs.

DOWN THE THROAT There are hairs in the nostrils that trap dirt and dust. Also, tiny particles such as germs stick to the mucus-covered lining inside the nasal chambers. So the air is filter-cleaned too, which does not happen if it is breathed in through the mouth. The mucus of the nasal lining is always being made. It usually passes back and down into the throat, perhaps helped by a sniff, and swallowed. If an infection by germs causes extra mucus, we remove this by blowing the nose.

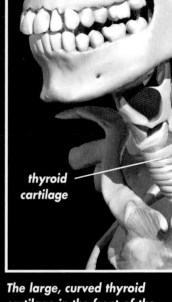

SOME FORMS OF AIR POLLUTION CAN be seen, like smoke and bits of floating powder or dust. But many harmful gases and fumes are unseen. They include the tiny particles from old vehicle engines, especially diesel engines.

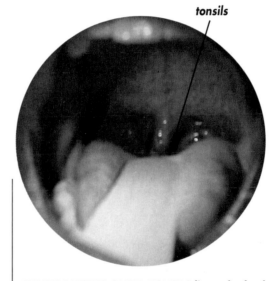

tonsils

LUMPY PATCHES CALLED TONSILS lie at the back of the throat. As parts of the disease-fighting immune system they may become swollen, red and painful during infection by germs.

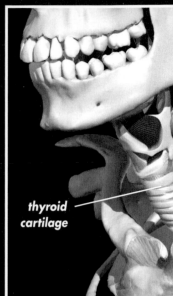

thyroid cartilage

The large, curved thyroid cartilage in the front of the upper neck, with two prongs facing up and down at each side, protects the lower throat, voice-box and windpipe.

SINUSES
Branching out from the nasal chamber are small passageways leading to four pairs of sponge-like, air-filled spaces. These are inside the skull bones around the face, and are called sinuses.

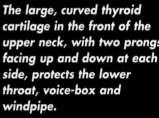

AH-TISH-OOOOOW!
A sneeze blasts air up the throat, through the nasal chambers and out of the nose. It happens when the nose is itchy or blocked, to clear the problem.

TRY IT YOURSELF
Speak normally, then while holding your nose. Your voice sounds very different. As you talk normally, sounds come out through the mouth and nose. The nasal chambers and the sinuses give the voice a fuller, richer sound. Holding your nose stops this.

If you have had to stay silent for a time – perhaps a 'sponsored silence' to raise money for a good cause – you know how important our voices are. We can send text messages, e-mails and posted letters. But the sounds made by the voicebox are our main means of communication with others.

IN THE NECK The voicebox, or larynx, is between the base of the throat and the upper part of the windpipe, or trachea. Its main structure is made of curved parts of cartilage, or 'gristle', which is similar to bone but slightly softer and more bendy or springy. The largest of these cartilages is called the thyroid cartilage, at the front. It makes a bulge under the skin in the front of the neck known as the 'Adam's apple'.

FOLDS NOT CORDS Two vocal cords are found in the larynx. They look like folds or ridges, one on either side, sticking out into the airway. Normally the vocal cords are apart so we can breathe without making a sound through the gap between them,

IN FOCUS
DOWN TO THE CHEST

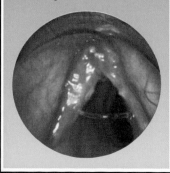

To speak or sing higher notes, the muscles in the voicebox pull the vocal cords and stretch them tighter, so they vibrate faster.

(known as the glottis). To make sounds, muscles pull the vocal cords almost together, leaving just a narrow gap. As air passes up from the lungs and through this gap it makes the vocal cords vibrate. These vibrations make the basic sounds of the voice. Our throat, mouth, nose chamber and sinuses make these noises louder, and the tongue, teeth and lips help us to produce clear speech.

Above the voicebox is the leaf-shaped flap of the epiglottis cartilage. When food is swallowed this folds down over the entrance to the voicebox, to prevent the food entering the airway and causing choking.

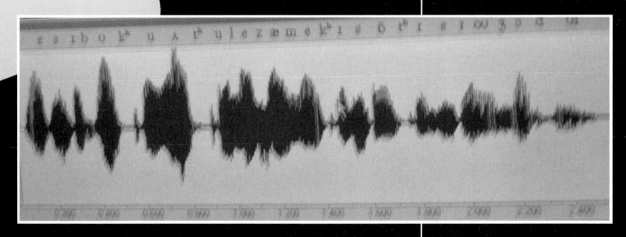

NO TWO PEOPLE HAVE EXACTLY THE SAME SHAPE OF VOICEBOX, throat, nose and mouth. So the sound of each person's voice is unique. A picture of the sound waves is called a sonogram or 'voiceprint'. It can be used like fingerprints to identify people for security reasons.

VOICEBOX

The voicebox is a chamber of complicated shape, made of cartilage, muscles and elastic-like, strap-shaped ligaments. The vocal cords are shaped like ridges.

 TRY IT YOURSELF

Feel your voicebox while humming, to detect the vibrations there. Make the hum louder and the vibrations become greater. Change your lip positions to make an 'eeee' and then 'oooo' and see how the mouth alters the basic sound of the vocal cords. Now make a hissing sound like a snake, and the voicebox vibrations stop. The hiss is from air passing through a narrow gap between the tongue and roof of the mouth.

INSTANT FACTS

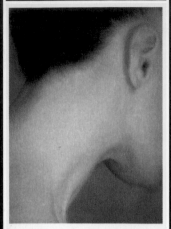

In an adult the windpipe has a **total length of 10–11 cm and is 1.5–2 cm wide**.

Its walls are strengthened with **16–20 C-shaped pieces of cartilage**.

The right main bronchus is **2.5 cm long**, and the left one nearer **5 cm in length**.

If all the different-sized air tubes in the lungs could be joined end to end **they would stretch more than 50 km**.

HEALTHWATCH

Some people have the condition called asthma, where breathing becomes difficult and wheezy. This has several causes. One is allergy or sensitivity to particles floating in the air, as in hay fever. The allergy causes the muscles in the airway walls to tighten, and the linings to make more mucus which stops air passing through.

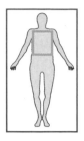

Every time you move your head and neck, you twist and bend your windpipe, or trachea. This is the main airway tube leading down to the chest.

HOLDING THE AIRWAYS OPEN The windpipe must keep itself open against the body's internal pressure. So its walls are strengthened with C-shaped pieces of springy cartilage ('gristle'). These make the windpipe very strong yet flexible and hold it open against the push of the parts around, allowing air to flow freely. At its base the windpipe divides into two slightly smaller tubes known as bronchi. One bronchus leads to each lung. Then the bronchus divides into smaller tubes, which also divide, and so on. All of these tubes have cartilage rings to keep them open too.

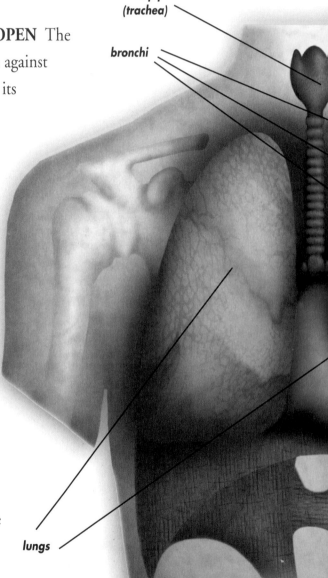

windpipe (trachea)

bronchi

lungs

TRY IT YOURSELF

Look in a mirror, and then turn your body to face left or right while your head stays looking at the mirror. See how the neck twists, with the windpipe inside, yet you can still breathe easily. Then give a small cough to 'clear your throat'. You are really clearing your lungs by coughing old mucus, with bits of dust and germs, up the windpipe and then swallowing it.

IN FOCUS
TREE IN THE CHEST

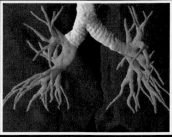

The branching pattern of air tubes in the lungs is known as the bronchial tree. Its narrowest 'twigs' (not shown here) extend into every part of each lung. The whole 'tree' sways and bends like a real one with each breath, as the lungs enlarge and deflate.

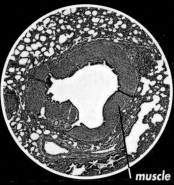

muscle

The walls of all but the smallest airways have a layer of smooth or involuntary muscle. This is designed to contract and narrow the airways automatically, in case of emergency, such as to keep out toxic fumes. But it can also contract due to an allergy such as asthma.

A BRONCHOSCOPE is a telescope-like device for looking down the throat into the windpipe and bronchi. It shows the strengthening pieces of cartilage and checks for blockages, infection by germs and other problems.

KEEPING CLEAN The windpipe, bronchi and bronchioles have a special 'self-clean' lining. Like the inside of the nose, the lining continuously makes a thin layer of sticky mucus to trap dust and germs. The lining is also filled with millions of tiny hairs called cilia, which push the mucus along, up the air tubes and windpipe to the throat, where it is regularly swallowed. This cleaning process keeps the lungs from becoming clogged up with dirt and germs.

HOUSE DUST MITES are tiny creatures which thrive in dust, carpets, curtains and beds. Their droppings dry into a powder that floats easily and, when breathed in, can cause the wheeziness of asthma.

THE WINDPIPE IS DIVIDES INTO TWO LARGE TUBES, which divide again to carry air deep into the lungs.

BRONCHIOLES

Starting with the windpipe and its division into the main bronchi, another 23 or so divisions result in thousands of tiny air tubes called bronchioles, deep in the lungs. When an asthma sufferer has an asthma attack, these airways contract, making it more difficult to breathe.

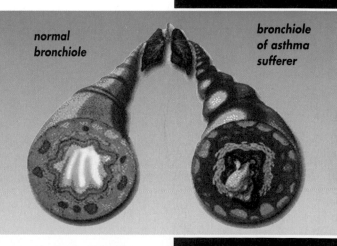

normal bronchiole

bronchiole of asthma sufferer

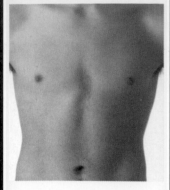

In both lungs of an adult there are about **300 million alveoli**.

If they were all flattened out their surface area would be about 50 sq metres when the lungs have breathed out, and up to 150 square metres when they breathe in.

The total area of the capillary blood vessels around all the alveoli is about 100 square metres.

◉ HEALTHWATCH

During breathing the millions of air sacs (alveoli) in the lungs inflate and deflate like tiny balloons. In the disease emphysema, caused by smoking cigarettes, these little air sacs become damaged. They become stiffer so don't bounce back so easily when breathing out, and their fragile walls break. This makes it much harder work to breathe. People with emphysema often become tired out after even the slightest exercise.

LUNGS DEEP IN THE LUNGS

Did you know that you have an area the size of a tennis court, wrapped and packed into your chest. This area is for taking in oxygen from the air, and its great size means that plenty of oxygen can be obtained, to keep the body alive.

FULL OF BUBBLES By the time the airways in the lungs have branched more than 20 times, they are thinner than hairs and number more than 10 million. Each of these tiny tubes is called a terminal bronchiole. At its end it has a bunch of bubble-shaped air spaces, looking like grapes on their stalk. The air spaces are called alveoli. The alveoli make up about one-half of the total volume of the lungs. The rest is made up from the various branching airways of the bronchi and bronchioles, and also two sets of branching blood vessels. These are the pulmonary arteries bringing low-oxygen blood from the heart, and pulmonary veins taking high-oxygen blood back again.

THE CAPILLARIES Like the airways, the pulmonary arteries divide and become smaller and smaller until they form the body's tiniest blood vessels, capillaries. A net-like set of capillaries surrounds each alveolus. The walls of the alveolus and the capillary are so thin, only 1/500th of one millimetre, that oxygen can easily pass from the air inside the alveolus, into the blood. At the same time the body's waste product carbon dioxide seeps the other way and is removed when the air is breathed out.

IN FOCUS
CHEST CONTENTS

airways

This illustration of the chest with the heart and lungs removed shows the branching airways and blood vessels within the breathing muscles of the rib cage.

IF THE INSIDE OF THE CHEST WAS ONE LARGE HOLLOW SPACE, it would have an area of less than half a square metre ~ far too small to take in enough oxygen to survive. The alveoli increase the area more than 100 times, to more than the area of a tennis court.

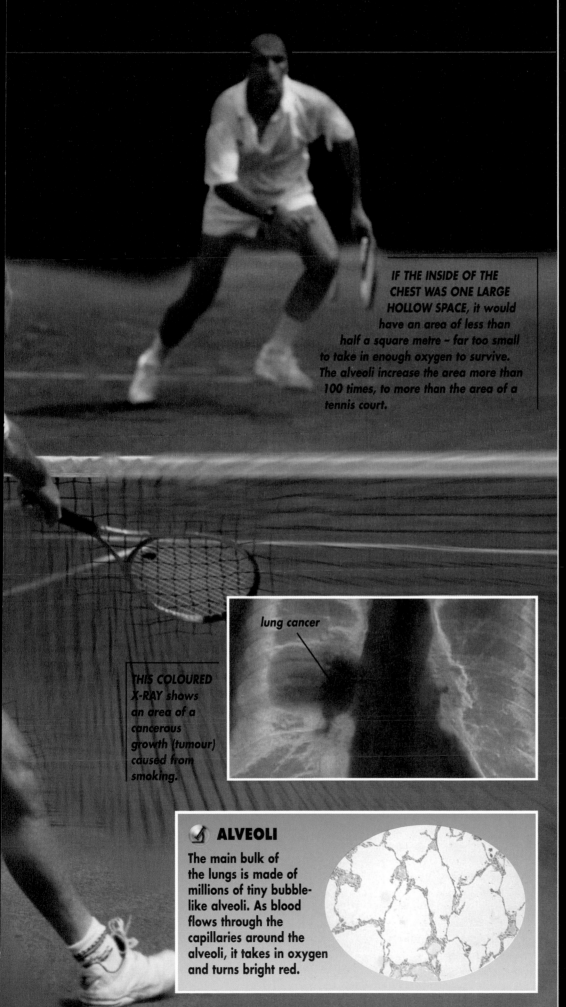

lung cancer

THIS COLOURED X-RAY shows an area of a cancerous growth (tumour) caused from smoking.

🖐 TRY IT YOURSELF

Hold a dangling paper tissue at arm's length. Aim a gentle blow at it, but with your mouth fairly wide open. See how much the tissue sways in the 'breeze'. Then make the same blowing effort but through a small hole between pursed lips. This forces the air out faster and harder, and the tissue should move more.

🖐 ALVEOLI

The main bulk of the lungs is made of millions of tiny bubble-like alveoli. As blood flows through the capillaries around the alveoli, it takes in oxygen and turns bright red.

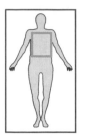

HEALTHWATCH

The respiratory system is one of the main ways that germs get into the body. Many are filtered out by nose hairs or trapped by mucus. But some pass through the delicate linings inside the nose, throat or lungs. They cause various infections, like colds and sore throats. Sneezing into a tissue or handkerchief avoids spreading them, otherwise tiny germ-carrying droplets can spray several metres.

LUNGS *BREATHING*

Breathing is one of the most basic actions of the human body. We can control it if we want to, like when we speak, swallow, suck a drink up a straw or blow our nose.

IN WITH THE FRESH AIR Like other body movements, breathing is muscle-powered. Normal breathing, at rest, involves two kinds of muscles. One is a curved sheet of muscle under the lungs, called the diaphragm. It is shaped like an upside-down bowl. When it tightens or contracts, it becomes flatter. This pulls down the bases of the lungs and so stretches the lungs bigger, sucking air down the windpipe into them. The other muscles are called intercostals and they are between the ribs. When they contract they make the ribs lift and swing out. This also stretches the lungs and sucks air into them.

OUT WITH THE STALE AIR Breathing in needs muscle effort, but breathing out does not. The lungs are stretched like elastic, and when the diaphragm and intercostal muscles relax, they spring back to their smaller size. This blows out the

LIKE OTHER FISH, LUNGFISH TAKE IN OXYGEN BY FRILLY GILLS under flap-like covers in the neck region. But they can also gulp air into a bag-like part near the stomach, which works like a lung. And they take in oxygen through their damp skin. So they can 'breathe' in three different ways!

BUSY MUSCLES NEED LOTS MORE OXYGEN, brought by the blood. So, the lungs breathe faster and deeper to take in this extra oxygen. Stooping slightly, with arms forward and down, makes deep breathing easier.

IN FOCUS
THE DIAPHRAGM

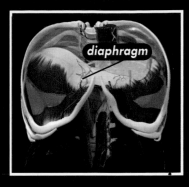

diaphragm

The diaphragm is a large, double-domed, sheet-shaped muscle at the base of the lungs. It forms the boundary between the thorax (chest) above it and the abdomen below. The gullet and major blood vessels pass through it.

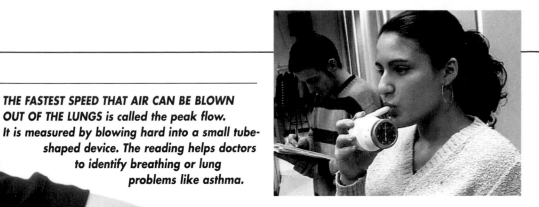

THE FASTEST SPEED THAT AIR CAN BE BLOWN OUT OF THE LUNGS is called the peak flow. It is measured by blowing hard into a small tube-shaped device. The reading helps doctors to identify breathing or lung problems like asthma.

stale air which contains less oxygen but more carbon dioxide from the lungs. The lungs are surrounded by two slippery, bag-like layers called the pleurae, which allow them to slide easily inside the chest as they get bigger and smaller with each breath.

TRY IT YOURSELF

Sit quietly for five minutes and then count the number of breaths in one minute. ('In' and 'out' counts as one breath.) Then jog or skip for two minutes, sit down, and count the rate again each minute for the next three minutes. How fast does your breathing rate return to normal? How do your friends compare?

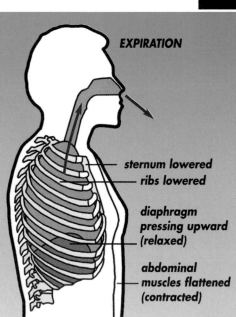

INSPIRATION

EXPIRATION

sternum raised
ribs raised
diaphragm flattened (contracted)
abdominal muscles relaxed

sternum lowered
ribs lowered
diaphragm pressing upward (relaxed)
abdominal muscles flattened (contracted)

FLEXIBLE LUNGS

The muscles of breathing, or respiration, expand the flexible lungs so that more air flows into them. These movements make the chest rise and fall with each breath. As the diaphragm flattens it also pushes the stomach and guts below it, making the belly bulge outwards.

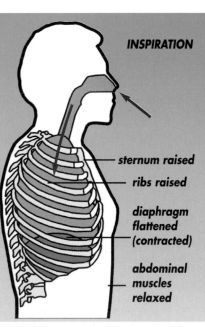

If the body was as big as a large city like London or New York, **its main blood vessels would be like motorways 150 metres across**, and its tiniest vessels would be about the width of a pencil.

The heart, blood and all the blood vessels make up about **one tenth of the weight of the whole body**.

If all the blood vessels in the body could be joined end to end, **they would go around the world more than twice**.

Our body has one bag-shaped muscle which we cannot relax, and which must keep working at all costs. This is the heart, the muscle-powered pump for the circulatory system. It beats every second to force blood through the network of blood vessels.

ROUND AND ROUND Our blood goes around and around, or circulates, through the body. It delivers oxygen to all body parts, organs and tissues. Blood also carries hundreds of other substances. These include energy-packed sugars, nutrients for growth, vitamins and minerals to keep the body working well, disease-fighting microscopic white cells, and the 'messenger' substances known as hormones which control many bodily processes.

ALWAYS BUSY Blood not only delivers – it collects too. It gathers up wastes for removal by other body parts. These are the two lungs, which get rid of the waste carbon dioxide, and the two kidneys, which filter unwanted substances from the blood to form the liquid urine. Blood also helps to keep our bodies at a regular temperature. It spreads heat from hard-working parts, like the heart and muscles, to cooler areas. If the body gets too hot, more blood flows through the skin and loses the extra warmth to the atmosphere.

ANY KIND OF MOVEMENT means muscles work harder, and need extra supplies of oxygen and energy. So the heart pumps harder and faster to increase blood flow through the muscles.

IN FOCUS
LOCATION OF THE HEART

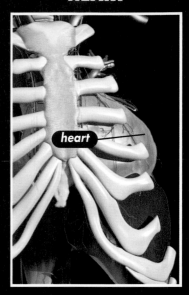

heart

The heart, shown here with its pale grey covering (the pericardium), is behind the breastbone.

THE BODY'S CIRCULATORY SYSTEM works like a giant production line. There are branches into every area, and vehicles come and go as they drop off fresh supplies and gather up wastes.

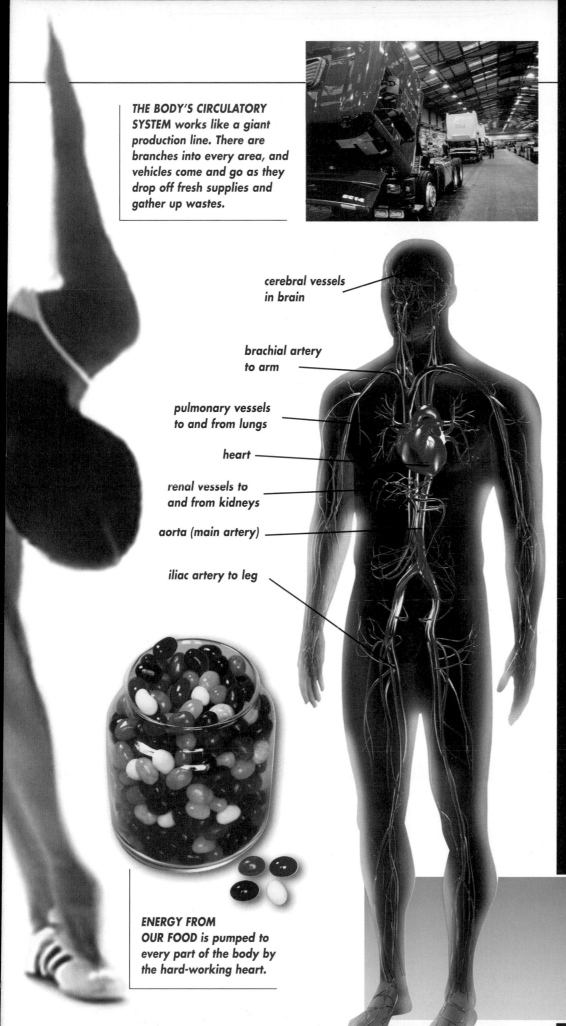

cerebral vessels in brain

brachial artery to arm

pulmonary vessels to and from lungs

heart

renal vessels to and from kidneys

aorta (main artery)

iliac artery to leg

ENERGY FROM OUR FOOD is pumped to every part of the body by the hard-working heart.

TRY IT YOURSELF

In a quiet place, put your fingers into your ears. You may be able to hear the sound of the blood flowing through them, pulsing with each beat of the heart. It makes a very deep thudding sound, like far-off thunder.

BLOOD VESSELS

The main blood vessels are named after the medical terms for the body parts they supply, such as the renal vessels leading to the kidneys.

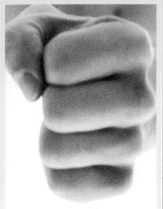

The heart is about **the size of its owner's clenched fist.**

In an average adult male the heart **weighs about 300 grams**, around the same as a medium grapefruit.

In **a typical woman** the heart weighs about 250 grams.

The lower-most pointed tip of **the heart is about level with the sixth rib.**

👁 HEALTHWATCH

In some of the world's wealthiest countries, heart and circulation problems are one of the leading causes of illness. Medical surveys show that habits to keep the heart healthy begin when young. They include avoiding eating too many fatty foods, especially animal fats, also avoiding too much salt, taking regular exercise and not smoking. It's never too early to begin living healthily!

HEART *THE HEART UP CLOSE*

'In love, your heart skips a beat'. The heart is a favourite subject of singers, writers and poets. Sadly their words are not really accurate. Love, courage and kindness come from the brain, not the heart. Yet even the clever brain relies on the heart to survive.

PEAR SHAPED The heart is not really 'heart'-shaped, as in cartoons about love. It is more like a squashed pear lying on its side. The heart is mainly a hollow bag with muscular walls, and inside are four hollow chambers. The two upper chambers, atria, are smaller with thin walls. The two lower chambers, ventricles, are much bigger with thick muscle walls. Each atrium connects to the ventricle below it through a flap-like valve. Blood flows into the heart via the atria and out of the heart via the ventricles.

THE TYPICAL CARTOON 'HEART' SHAPE IS A USEFUL SYMBOL, but not accurate. The human heart is shaped more like a squashed pear or pointy-ended potato.

PUMP, PUMP, PUMP, hour after hour, year by year. Mechanical pumps last 10 or even 20 years. The human heart continues for 70, 80, even 100 years.

IN FOCUS
INSIDE THE HEART

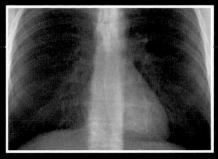

TWO IN ONE The heart is not a single pump. Rather, it is two pumps side by side. The right pump has one upper atrium and one lower ventricle. Low-oxygen blood comes into the right atrium from all around the body, passes through the valve into the ventricle, and flows from there out to the lungs. High-oxygen blood returning from the lungs enters the left atrium, goes through the valve to the left ventricle, and then flows out all around the body. So the body really has two circulations. The short one to the lungs and back is the pulmonary circulation, the long one all around the body is the systemic circulation.

THERE ARE SEVERAL WAYS OF SEEING THE HEART WITHIN THE BODY.
The most common is a chest X-ray. The heart in the X-ray above appears pink. A coronary angiogram outlines the heart's own blood vessels, and an echocardiogram shows its beating motion 'live'.

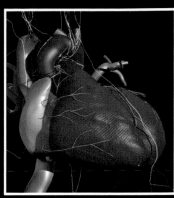

The muscle that makes up the walls of the heart, called cardiac muscle or myocardium, never ceases working and needs a continuing supply of blood.

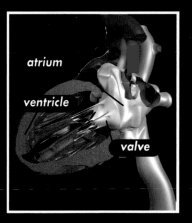

atrium

ventricle

valve

On each side of the heart the small upper chamber, the atrium, receives blood and passes it through a valve to the main lower chamber, the ventricle. This pushes the blood out into the blood vessels.

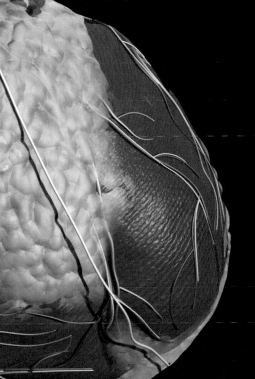

🖐 TRY IT YOURSELF

Next time you lie on your back to rest or sleep, look at your chest. You can probably see its breathing movements, but not the heart's motion. However, your abdomen ('tummy') may rise and fall slightly with each heartbeat, as blood pumps into the large vessels inside.

ALMOST ALL KINDS OF ANIMALS HAVE A HEART-LIKE PUMPING ORGAN for body fluids. Usually there is just the one, but the earthworm possesses five in a row along its main blood vessel.

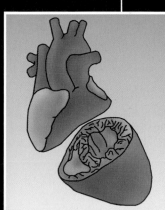

🔬 CHAMBERS

A slice through the middle of the heart shows how the smaller right ventricle, sending blood to the lungs, has thinner walls and a curved shape compared to the left ventricle, which pumps blood bodywide.

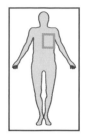

The heart beats almost every second, without you even noticing it. When the body is relaxed, a heartbeat is slow and steady, but when the body is active, the heartbeat gets faster and harder, and you feel it pounding inside your chest.

BLOOD IN Each heartbeat is a smooth, continuous motion. First, the heart muscle relaxes and blood oozes from the main blood vessels into the upper chambers – the atrial. Their thin walls bulge easily. Next, the muscle in each atrial wall gets shorter or contracts. Like a stretched balloon contracting, this squeezes the blood inside the atria and pushes it through the funnel-shaped valve into the ventricle.

IF FRIGHTENED, WE FEEL THE HEART POUNDING FASTER and harder. It is responding to nerve signals from the brain, and also the hormone (message-carrying chemical) adrenaline in the blood.

✋ TRY IT YOURSELF

When the body is relaxed, the heart rate is usually 70 beats or less each minute. To find out your pulse, put your first and second fingers on the inside of your wrist and press gently. Count the number of beats every 15 seconds, multiply that number by four and you will have your heart rate in beats per minute.

IN FOCUS
HEART VALVES

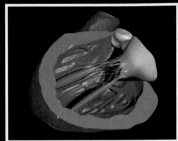

The valves from the upper to lower chambers are called the tricuspid (right side) and bicuspid or mitral (left side). They are made of a tough, leathery material shaped like a funnel, held open by cords.

THE HEARTBEAT IS CAUSED BY TINY ELECTRICAL SIGNALS passing through its muscle. The signals can be detected by sensors on the chest, and shown as a spiky line – the ECG (electrocardiograph).

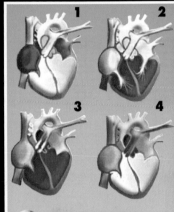

🫀 HEART BEATS

After the atria fill (1), they contract and the valves open (2), to allow blood through to the ventricles. The valves shut when the ventricles contract to stop blood flowing back (3). The valves open as the ventricles contract and blood rushes out into the arteries (4). The sounds of the valves opening and closing make the sound of each heartbeat, 'lub-dup'.

BLOOD OUT

Next, the thicker muscle in the wall of the ventricle contracts, squeezing the blood much harder. This makes the valve into the atrium slap shut, so the blood cannot return there. Instead it flows out through another valve into the main blood vessels – on its way to the lungs from the heart's right side, and around the body from the left side. Then the heart relaxes again, and so the whole process continues.

ONLY RARELY DOES THE HUMAN HEART go as fast as 200 beats each minute. Smaller animals have faster heart rates than us. The tiny shrew's heart, which is smaller than a peanut, beats 1,000 times each minute!

Blood makes up about one twelfth of the weight of the body.

In an average woman, the volume of blood is 4–5 litres.

In a typical man, the volume is 5–6 litres.

At any one moment, only ¹⁄₂₀ **th of the body's blood is in the capillaries.** Most, around three-quarters, is in the veins.

When blood clots in a blood vessel, heart chamber or other site within the body, this is called thrombosis. The clot itself is a thrombus.

◉ HEALTHWATCH

Do you know your blood group? There are two main sets of groups, ABO and rhesus +/- (positive/ negative). They show how blood reacts if mixed with blood from another person. If someone has an accident and needs replacement blood, called a transfusion, the groups must be suited or 'matched'. If not matched, the added blood will clot, clog vessels, and cause serious medical problems— and sometimes even death.

BLOOD *LIQUID FOR LIFE*

Blood is red, thick, sticky, sweet, sealing, healing - and essential for life. It would take many books like this to describe all of the hundreds of substances in blood, and all of the jobs they do.

WHY RED? Blood goes bright red when it contains plenty of oxygen. The oxygen is attached to a substance in blood known as haemoglobin, which gives the red colour. Haemoglobin is found in one of blood's main contents, the tiny red cells. A drop of blood as big as this letter 'o' contains 25 million red cells. They pick up oxygen in the lungs and the blood turns bright red. Then in the capillaries the oxygen passes from the red cells, out to the tissues around. As this happens the colour from bright red to darker reddish purple.

FULL OF GOODNESS Blood contains other kinds of cells too. The main ones are white cells which clean the blood and fight disease. There are also parts of cells called platelets. At a cut or injury, these platelets clump together and the blood goes thicker and sticky. The result is a lump called a clot, which seals the cut and stops more blood leaking away. In addition blood carries energy in the form of glucose or 'blood sugar', for use by muscles.

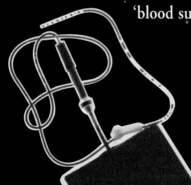

SOME CROPS ARE GROWN HYDROPONICALLY, *without soil. The water around their roots contains all the nutrients and minerals they need. Blood is similar, carrying all the substances needed by every body part.*

VAST AMOUNTS OF STORED BLOOD ARE USED EVERY DAY by hospitals and medical centres, for people who are ill, injured or having surgery. Giving or donating this blood is very valuable - *it can save a life.*

IN FOCUS
WOUND HEALING

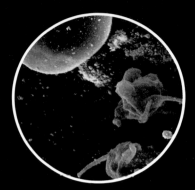

SOMETIMES INJURIES ARE TOO BIG FOR BLOOD TO SEAL BY CLOTTING. They need an emergency covering like a bandage to press on the part, slow down blood loss and keep out germs.

When we suffer a wound, within seconds the damage causes sticky micro-threads of the substance fibrin to appear in the blood. Red cells and platelets get tangled in them and the platelets produce more sticky substances and threads. Eventually a clot forms that plugs the gap.

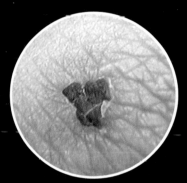

Over a few days the clot hardens into a scab, which protects the area while the damaged parts grow again.

🖐 TRY IT YOURSELF

In a safe place, carefully whirl one arm around like a windmill a few times. Quickly hold both hands together and compare their colours. The force of whirling causes blood to flow down the arm but not back up, so the whirled hand becomes redder.

🔬 BLOOD CONTENT

Just over half of blood is plasma, which is a watery liquid containing hundreds of dissolved substances like sugars, minerals and body salts. Most of the rest of the blood is made up of red cells.

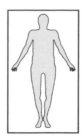

Blood does not slosh around the body like water in a barrel. It flows through a network of tubes called blood vessels. There are three main kinds of vessels – each different in size and structure.

WAVE OF PRESSURE Blood vessels leading from the heart are known as arteries. The largest are about the width of a thumb. Arteries have thick walls, which are very tough and stretchy. Blood comes out of the heart in a surge of pressure, and this makes the artery walls bulge. As this high-pressure surge travels out into the artery network, all of the arteries around the body bulge with it.

TOO SMALL TO SEE As arteries divide they become narrower and their walls get thinner. They lead to all body parts, including the heart itself. Finally they divide into the smallest kinds of vessels, capillaries. The walls of a capillary are so thin that oxygen and other substances can seep through them from the blood inside, to the cells and tissues around. Waste substances move the other way, into the blood.

WIDE AND FLOPPY Capillaries join to make wider vessels, veins. These take the blood back to the heart. By the time the blood has gone through the arteries and capillaries, it has lost most of its pressure. So the vein walls are thin and floppy, and blood flows through them much more slowly.

TO BLOW UP A BALLOON, you need high air pressure. The surge of blood pressure from a heartbeat makes balloon-like bulges which travel along the walls of the arteries.

TUNNELS CARRY CARGO AND SUPPLIES QUICKLY PAST AN OBSTRUCTION, like a mountain or river. Arteries do the same, carrying blood swiftly past other body parts until they reach their intended destination.

📖 INSTANT FACTS

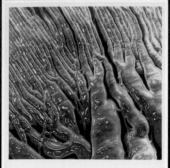

The body's main artery, the aorta, is about **25 mm wide** and blood surges through it at 30 cm each second.

A typical smaller **artery is 5 mm wide** and blood flows along at 5 cm per second.

A **capillary is just 1–2 mm long** and only $\frac{1}{25}$th mm wide.

A large vein is 30 mm wide and its **blood moves very slowly**, less than 1 mm per second.

👁 HEALTHWATCH

The heart has its own blood vessels, coronary arteries and veins. If the coronary arteries become stiff and clogged up, the blood cannot get through and the heart muscle becomes short of oxygen. The result is chest pain, sweating and breathlessness, in the condition called angina. A more serious blockage causes a heart attack.

IN FOCUS
BLOOD VESSELS

A CAPILLARY IS SO THIN that even the smallest cells in the body, blood's red cells (see p. 28), have to pass along them in single file.

CHEMICAL FACTORIES AND OIL REFINERIES ARE A MAZE OF pipes, tubes, ducts, vessels and channels. But this is nothing compared to the body's network of blood vessels, which would be like a giant factory 50 km long.

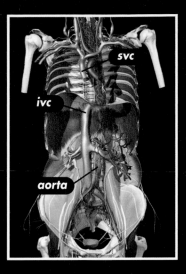

Branches off the central main artery, the aorta, go to the head, arms, abdomen and legs. The main vein returning to the heart from the upper body is the superior vena cava (svc), and from the lower body, inferior vena cava (ivc).

☝ TRY IT YOURSELF

Look at blood vessels, on yourself or an older family member. The veins on the inside of the wrist and forearm are just under the thin skin there. See how the veins come together as they carry blood back up the arm to the heart.

⚓ ARTERIES UP CLOSE

Most of an artery's wall is muscle. Under the brain's control, the muscle can contract to make the artery narrower, and so reduce blood flow to the part it supplies. A capillary is five times thinner than a human hair, and shorter than this 'i'. Its walls are just one cell thick. A vein is wide and flexible, with very thin walls. The main veins have flap-like valves to make sure the low-pressure, slow-flowing blood goes the correct way, back to the heart.

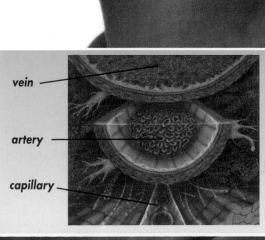

vein

artery

capillary

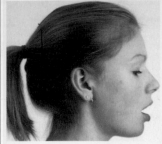

An average adult body contains **around one to two litres of lymph.**

Lymph flows very slowly, less than one millimetre each second.

Lymph nodes range in size from **as small as a rice grain to as large as a big grape.**

The **main groups of lymph nodes** are in **the neck, armpits, groin and inside the lower body**.

During an infection, lymph nodes swell with extra **white cells,** dead germs and body fluids, to be **larger than tennis balls.**

HEALTHWATCH

Around the world, billions of people are protected from infections by immunisation. Versions of the germs are put into the body. The immune defence system learns to recognise and fight them. Later, if the real germs invade, the defences kill them before they can multiply. This process is called immunisation.

BLOOD *Fighting Diseases*

Germs are everywhere - in air, water and soil and on almost every object. But the body fights a silent, never-ending war against them, and lucky for us, usually wins. The invisible armies which defend us against germs and disease make up the immune system.

CELLS TO THE RESCUE Some of the best 'soldiers' in the immune system are white cells, with thousands in every drop of blood. There are different kinds. Some attack germs directly, 'eating' them whole. Others make natural body substances called antibodies which stick onto germs so that they die. Still others take in any bits of waste and rubbish to keep the blood clean. White cells can move out of the blood and into other body parts, especially into the mysterious clear fluid called lymph.

PEOPLE ARE CHECKED AS THEY ENTER A COUNTRY, to make sure they are not intending harm. The body's immune system is constantly on guard and carries out similar checks for 'terrorist' germs.

In a vaccination or 'jab', germs which have been made harmless may be put into the body, to make the body resistant or immune to the real germs (see Healthwatch).

IN FOCUS
MORE BODY DEFENDERS

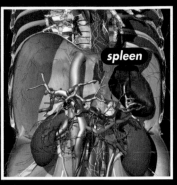

spleen

The dark-red spleen stores blood, recycles old red cells and makes new white cells.

THE 'OTHER' CIRCULATION Like blood, lymph is a liquid that flows around the body. But it has a different set of tubes, called lymph vessels. Lymph begins as the general fluid around and between body cells, tissue and other parts. It collects in small tubes that join to form larger lymph vessels. In some parts the vessels widen to form lymph nodes. These are packed with white cells and other disease-fighters. If germs invade, the lymph nodes enlarge as the white cells multiply and go on the attack. We call these enlarged lymph nodes 'swollen glands'.

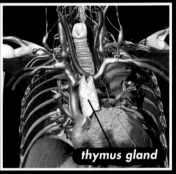

thymus gland

The pale-coloured thymus gland helps to 'train' white cells to recognize germs, especially in childhood.

THE LYMPH VESSELS COLLECT LYMPH FLUID FROM ALL AROUND THE BODY.
The main vessels, lymphatics, join the blood system near the heart, where the lymph fluid is added to the blood stream.

🖐 TRY IT YOURSELF

Have you ever had a 'stitch'? This is a sharp pain in the upper left side, often during exercise which the body normally does not do. The pain may come from the spleen. This tightens or contracts to pour its stores of blood into the blood stream, to help with carrying oxygen for the muscles.

🔬 VESSELS AND NODES

Lymph fluid flows much more slowly than blood. It has no pump of its own. It is squeezed along by the pressure of general body movements. Valves in the main lymph vessels make sure the fluid flows the correct way. Inside a typical lymph node or 'gland' (right) are compartments full of lymph fluid and many kinds of white blood cells.

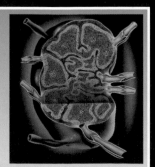

GLOSSARY

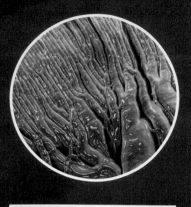

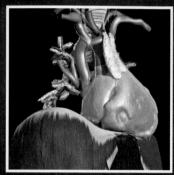

ABDOMEN The lower main body, from the base of the chest down to the hips.

ALLERGY A bodily process that resembles the defence reaction to harmful germs or toxins, caused by substances like plant pollen grains or house dust.

ALVEOLI Microscopic bubble-shaped air sacs in the lungs, where oxygen passes from air into the blood.

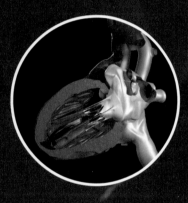

ARTERIOLE A type of blood vessel carrying blood away from the heart into organs and tissue, thinner than an artery but not as narrow as a capillary.

ARTERY Strong, thick-walled main blood vessel that carries blood away from the heart. Note: Not all arteries carry bright red, high-oxygen blood. The pulmonary arteries to the lungs convey dark, low-oxygen, 'blue' blood.

ATRIUM One of the two small upper chambers of the heart, which receives blood flowing in from the veins and passes it to the ventricle below.

BRONCHI The larger airways in the chest, which branch from the base of the windpipe (trachea).

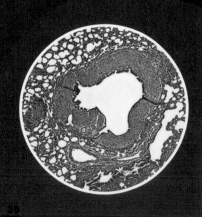

BRONCHIOLES Air tubes in the chest, narrower than bronchi but not as thin as terminal bronchioles.

CAPILLARY The thinnest, shortest type of blood vessel, far too narrow to see with the unaided eye.

CARBON DIOXIDE A waste product made inside the body, by releasing the energy from food substances, which is carried in the blood and then passes into the air in the lungs, to be breathed out.

CARTILAGE A strong, smooth, shiny, slightly bendy substance, sometimes called 'gristle', that forms body parts like the nose, ears and voicebox, and covers the ends of bones in a joint.

CELLS Tiny parts or building-blocks of the body, which in their billions make up larger parts like bones, muscles and skin.

CILIA Tiny hair-like projections of microscopic cells, found in many body parts. Cilia in the lining of the airways wave or 'beat' to keep its covering of sticky, germ-gathering mucus on the move, up and out of the lungs.

DIAPHRAGM A large sheet of muscle, shaped like a double-dome, at the base of the chest under the lungs.

INVOLUNTARY MUSCLE The muscle of inner parts like the lung, airways and guts, also called unstriated or visceral muscle, which we cannot control at will.

LARYNX Name for the voicebox area.

MUSCLE A body part specialised to get shorter, or contract.

NASAL CHAMBERS The air spaces inside the nose, through which air passes as we breathe in and out.

OXYGEN A gas with no colour, taste or smell, that makes up one-fifth of air. It is needed by the body to release the energy from food substances, especially blood sugar or glucose.

PHARYNX Name for the throat area. (A sore throat is known as pharyngitis.)

PLAQUE In blood vessels, a lump of fatty substance that forms in the lining, like 'fur' in a water pipe, and which narrows or even blocks the vessel.

PLEURAE Smooth, slippery, bag-like layers that wrap around the lungs and allow them to change size with the movements of breathing.

RESPIRATION 1: For the whole body, breathing air in and out to obtain oxygen and get rid of carbon dioxide. 2: In a cell, the chemical breakdown of blood sugar or glucose, using oxygen, to release its energy (cellular respiration).

SINUSES Honeycomb-like air spaces within the skull bones around the face,

connected to the main airway in the nose by openings or ducts.

TERMINAL BRONCHIOLES The thinnest air tubes in the lungs, which end at groups of microscopic air sacs, alveoli.

THORAX The chest region, from the neck and shoulders down to the abdomen, which contains the heart and main blood vessels, and the lungs and main airways.

TRACHEA Name for the windpipe, extending from the base of the voicebox (larynx) down to the site where it branches into two smaller airways, the bronchi.

VENTRICLE One of the two large lower chambers of the heart, which receives blood flowing into it from the atrium above, and pumps it out into the arteries.

VENULE A type of blood vessel carrying blood from organs and tissues towards the heart, wider than a capillary but not as large as a vein.

VOCAL CORDS Small flaps or ridges in the voicebox, which shake very fast or vibrate to make the sounds of the voice.

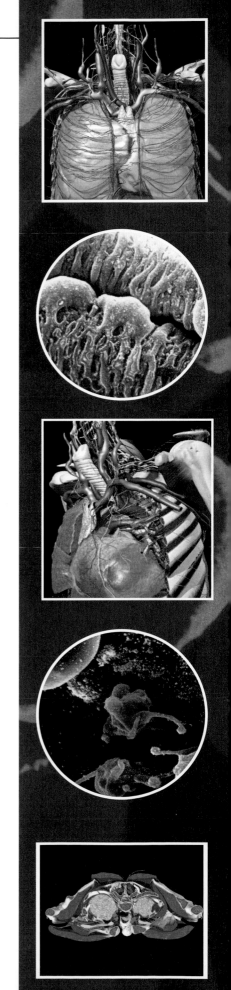

I N D E X

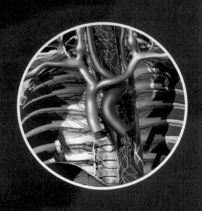

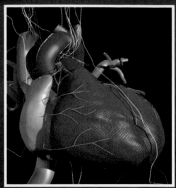

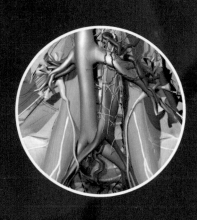

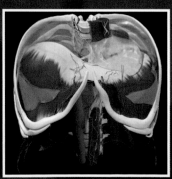

Copyright © ticktock Entertainment Ltd 2004
First published in Great Britain in 2004 by ticktock Media Ltd.,
Unit 2, Orchard Business Centre, North Farm Road, Tunbridge Wells, Kent, TN2 3XF
We would like to thank: Elizabeth Wiggans and Jenni Rainford for their help with this book.
ISBN 1 86007 562 2 HB   ISBN 1 86007 558 4 PB
Printed in China
A CIP catalogue record for this book is available from the British Library.

Picture Credits: Alamy: OFCl, 5tl, 9tc, 9c and 9bc, 12tl, 13c, 14-15c, 15c, 18tl, 19tc, 19cr, 20bc, 21tc, 22-23c, 24bc, 25c, 25tr and cr, 26bc, 27 tl, 28b. Mediscan: 12-13c, 13t. Primal Pictures: OFCr, 7tr, 9tr, 11tr, 13tr, 15tr, 17tr, 19tr, 20-21c, 21tr, 21cr, 23tr, 27 tr, 29tr, 29cr. Science Photo Library: 4 all, 9br, 11c, 13cr, 15bc, 17tc, 19c, 23cr, 26tl, 27tc, 27b, 29-30c, 29br, 30tl.

TRAVEL INSIDE THE BODY FROM THE LUNGS TO THE HEART

The human body is the most incredible machine on the planet. But have you ever wondered how it all works?

IN THIS BOOK, FIND OUT WHY YOU:

- **SNEEZE** and sniff when you feel unwell
- Have a **HEART** that never stops beating
- Have blood that is **BRIGHT RED**
- Rely on your **LIVER AND KIDNEYS** to keep you healthy
- Call on a **SPECIAL ARMY** inside you to fight off deadly diseases

Packed with *diagrams* to explain complicated processes, *illustrations* taken from a digital model of the anatomy and *simple experiments* for you to try out yourself.

The Body Atlas series explains, in easy-to-understand language, how the human body works, and relates that information to everyday activities and situations that children will recognise. Linked to the National Curriculum Key Stage 2.

SUITABLE FOR AGES 8+